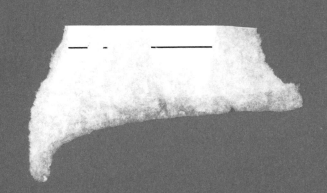

SCIENCE
in Action
MY SENSES

Hearing

Sally Hewitt

Publisher: Maxime Boucknooghe
Editorial Director: Victoria Garrard
Art Director: Miranda Snow
Series Editor: Claudia Martin
Series Designer: Bruce Marshall
Photographer: Michael Wicks
Consultant: Kristina Routh

First published in the UK in 2016 by
QED Publishing
Part of The Quarto Group
The Old Brewery, 6 Blundell Street
London, N7 9BH

A catalogue record for this book is available from
the British Library.

ISBN 978 1 78493 468 2

Printed in China

Picture credits
t = top, b = bottom, c = centre, l = left, r = right,
fc = front cover

Corbis 8t Alain Nogues, 10b Tom Stewart, 12l Pat
Doyle, 12r Norbert Schaefer, 13 ROB & SAS, 18 Jim
Craigmyle
Getty Images 4 Elyse Lewin/Photographers Choice,
5t Richard Price/Taxi, 5b Chris Windsor/The Image Bank,
6b Romily Lockyer/The Image Bank, 8b Macchina
Stone, 9t David Tipling/Photographers Choice
Shutterstock fc Patrick Foto/Sponner/DK Arts/ Yegor
Larin/Ivonne Wierink, 5r Alexandr III, 10t Netta07, 12l
Alexandr III, 20t and r wckiw

Words in **bold** can be
found in the glossary
on page 22.

Contents

Hear this

You have five main senses that give you information about the world around you.

The fives senses are sight, touch, smell, taste and hearing.

This book is about hearing.

◀ Hearing helps you to listen and understand what people say.

Your sense of hearing can warn you of danger. An emergency vehicle has a **loud** siren. It means...

Careful! Stay out of the way!

We also use our hearing to listen to music. What music do you like?

What other sounds do you like to hear?

World of sound

The world around you is full of sounds. What can you hear now?

▲ You use your **ears** to hear.

Now close your eyes and listen. Can you hear any new sounds?

Try putting a shell to your ear. Can you hear the air moving inside? Does it sound like the sea?

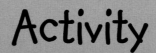

Activity

Try using your sense of hearing to guess what is happening around you.

Close your eyes and ask a friend to:

- Pour water into a glass
- Clap their hands
- Tear a piece of paper
- Bite an apple

Can you guess what your friend is doing by the sounds they make?

Sound waves

You can hear when **sound waves** go into your ears.

When a helicopter is in the sky, its blades move the air around them and make sound waves.

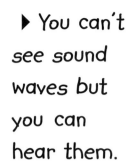 You can't see sound waves but you can hear them.

Sound waves have different patterns. When the sound waves enter your ears, your ears send a message to your brain. Your brain tells you what you are hearing.

Eardrums

Your **eardrum** is an important part of your ear. It is a thin flap of skin which is stretched tightly like a drum.

When you bang a drum, the skin **vibrates**. When sound waves go into your ears, they make your eardrum vibrate.

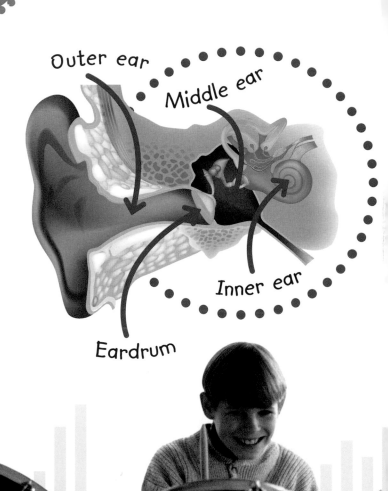

Outer ear

Middle ear

Inner ear

Eardrum

These vibrations move the tiny bones in your middle ear. These vibrations travel to the inner ear and the sound message is then sent to your brain!

Activity

Make some sound waves!

- Stretch cling film over a bowl. (This is like your eardrum.)

- Sprinkle rice on top.

- Bang a baking tray with a spoon.

- Watch the sound waves make the cling film vibrate and the rice jump.

Loud and quiet

Sounds make different vibrations in the air. Loud sounds make very big vibrations. Quiet sounds make small vibrations.

Loud sounds can hurt your ears! You can put your hands over your ears to keep out some of the sound.

◀ A trumpet can sound very loud! What other loud sounds are there?

You have to listen carefully to hear quiet sounds. You can hear quiet sounds better if they are close to your ear.

▼ Whispering is a quiet sound. What other quiet sounds are there?

Where's that sound?

Your ears are shaped a bit like **funnels** to catch sounds.

◀ You can make the funnel bigger by cupping your hand behind your ear.

Animals have differently shaped ears. Some animals can hear **better** than you.

▶ This dog can turn its ears quickly towards a sound without moving its head!

Activity

You can usually tell where someone is by listening to the sounds they make.

Try this game:

- Ask a friend to shut his or her eyes. Tiptoe around them, then stop and make a tiny squeak.

- Can your friend point to where you are by listening?

- Does the game get harder if you play some soft music in the background?

Near and far

If you are near a moving car, it can sound very loud! But the sound becomes quieter as the car moves further away.

Sound waves spread out as they travel through the air, and become quieter.

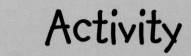

Activity

Sound can travel through different materials like string. Try this!

- Make a hole in the bottom of two plastic cups.

- Thread a long piece of string through each hole and tie a knot at the end inside the cup.

- Give a cup to a friend and pull the string tight.

- Talk into one cup. Your friend will hear your voice through the cup at the other end.

High and low

Musical instruments can play **high** and **low** notes depending on how they vibrate.

The thick strings on a guitar play low notes.

The thin strings on a guitar play higher notes.

◀ The strings on a guitar vibrate and play different notes.

Activity

You can play high and low notes with a glass of water.

- Pour yourself a glass of water.

- Tap the glass gently with a spoon and listen to the sound.

- Have a drink. Tap the glass again.

- How has the sound changed?

- Tap every time you have a drink.

Does the note get higher or lower?

Being deaf

People who can't hear use other senses such as sight.

Some deaf and hearing people use **sign language**. They make signs with their hands to talk to each other.

Sorry

Thank you

People can also learn to understand what someone is saying or feeling by looking at their face and lips.

There are lots of ways to tell a story without speaking or listening. What story could this boy be telling?

Eardrum

A small piece of skin inside your ear. It is like a drum skin.

Ears

You have two ears. They are the parts of your body you hear with.

Funnel

A funnel is wide at the top and narrower at the bottom.

High

Sounds can be high. A bird singing makes a high sound.

Loud

Sounds can be loud. A road drill makes a loud sound.

Low

Sounds can be low. A dog growling makes a low sound.

Quiet

Sounds can be quiet. Whispering is a quiet sound.

Sign language

Using your hands, face and body to talk to people.

Sound waves

Sounds travel through the air in sound waves.

Vibrate

To move backwards and forwards a tiny amount very fast.

INDEX

23